Little Sun

A Wild West Story

For the Kids Cabin Crew

By Jamie Boot

Copyright © Jamie Boot 2024

Many years ago in the Wild Wild West,
In the days of cowboys and shooting contests,

Was a cowgirl called Annie who had the best shot,
Armed with her super soaker always hitting the spot.

One hot day while riding her horse,
Through mountains and deserts with her water gun of course,

SALOON

SHOOT
CONTEST
DETAILS
INSIDE

She stopped at a saloon for a well earned drink,
When she noticed a sign that made her think.

SHOOTING
MATCH

ONLY THE BEST
IN THE WEST
NEED APPLY!

ON
THANKSGIVING
DAY

AT
CINCINNATI
PARK

She read out loud with a WOOF and a BARK,
"A shooting contest next week at the park!"
The sheriff piped up, who was listening in,
"You can win that Annie," he said with a grin.

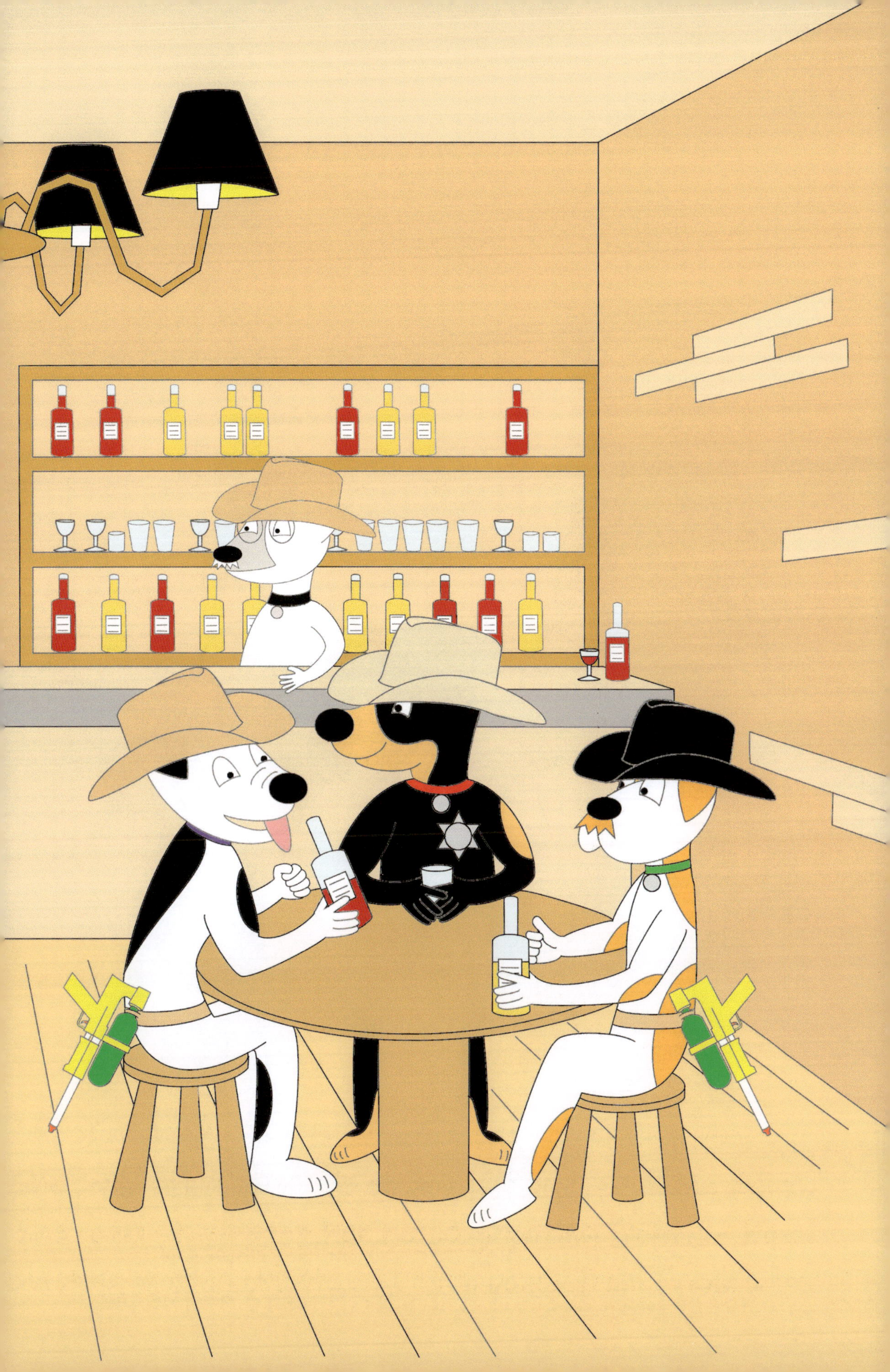

SHOOTING
MATCH

ONLY THE BEST
IN THE WEST
NEED APPLY!

ON
THANKSGIVING
DAY

AT
CINCINNATI
PARK

Just at that moment, a bandit showed up,
"You're under arrest!" the sheriff yelled at the pup.

The bandit looked scared and ran out of the door,
The sheriff gave chase, shouting "Come Annie!" with a ROAR!

Across the frontier they chased the bad pup,
Until Annie declared "Thats it, times up!"

She grabbed her rifle and shot from short range,
Drenching the bandit, leaving him very deranged.

"Well done Annie!" the sheriff cried out,
"It's straight to the jailhouse for that pup no doubt,
That baddie has been an enormous pest,
Now get yourself home and enter the contest!"

It was the day of the shoot and the targets were set,
A marksman named Frank was the bookies best bet,
Frank was charming, a real nice guy,
He took his first shot and hit the bullseye!

Annie was next, focused and alert,
She pulled the trigger and let out a squirt,

The shot was good, it could never miss,
It smashed the target, Frank blew
her a kiss!

On and on this went, twenty-four times,
The sheriff had to leave to investigate more crimes,

Then on his next go, Frank shot wide,
He lost the competition but was happy inside.

Annie said to Frank, "Why are you so pleased?"
"Can I take you for dinner?" said Frank on his knees,
The couple got married, they travelled near and far,
Winning competitions with Annie as the star.

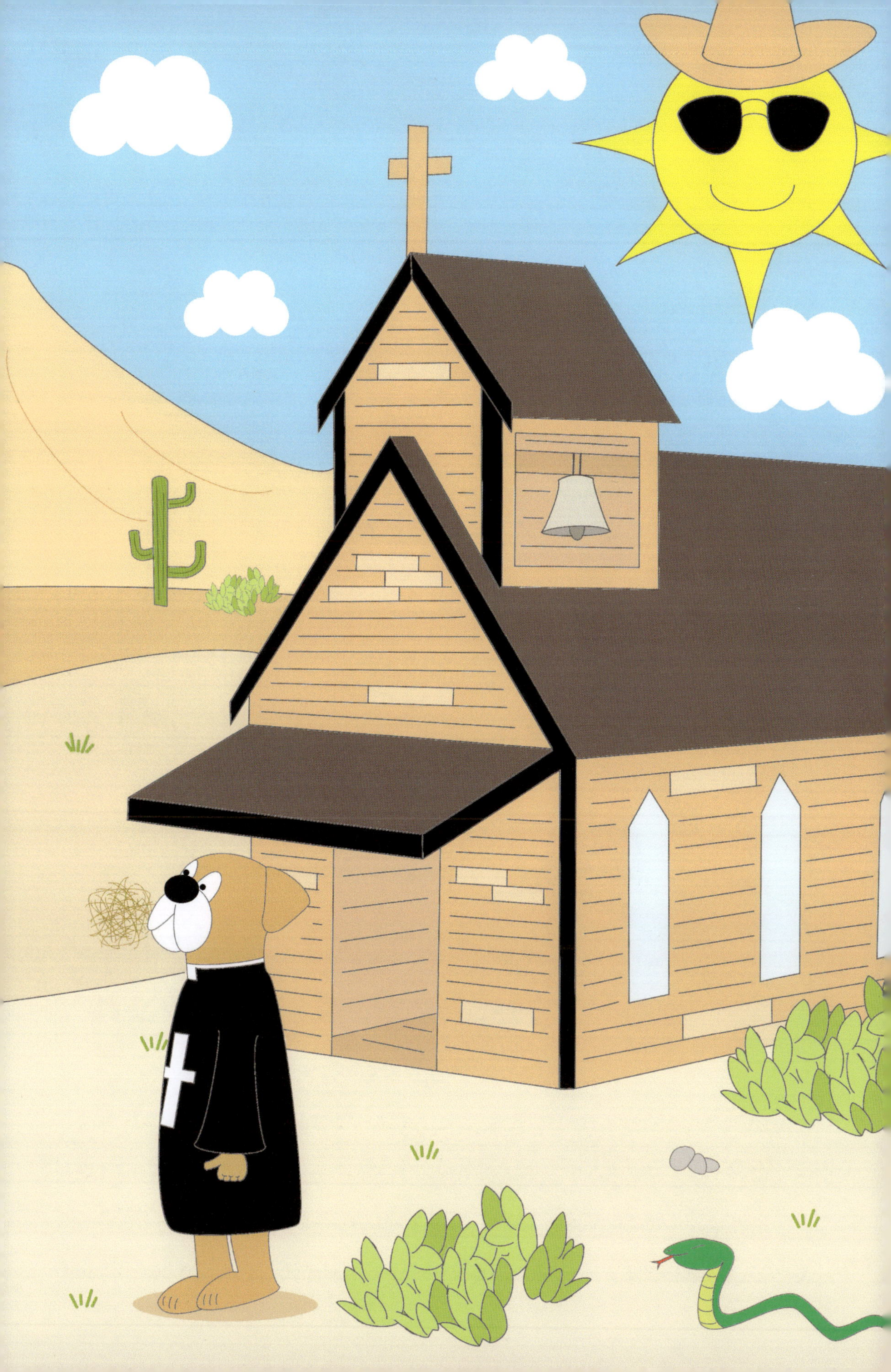

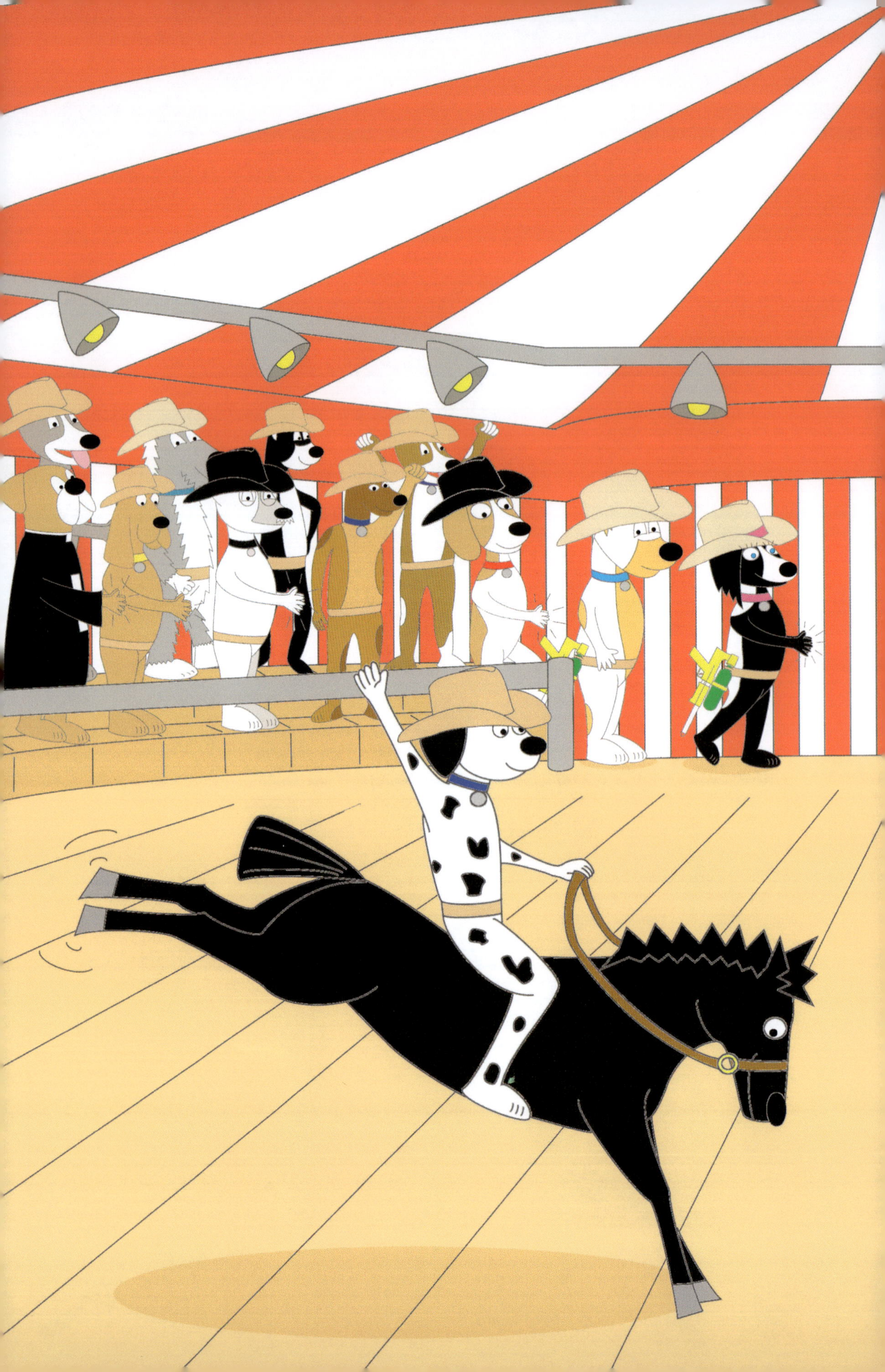

The double act was famous and it wasn't long until,
They joined the wild west show, hosted by Buffalo Bill,
Bill's show was awesome, full of happy faces,
With acts like bronco riding and even running races!

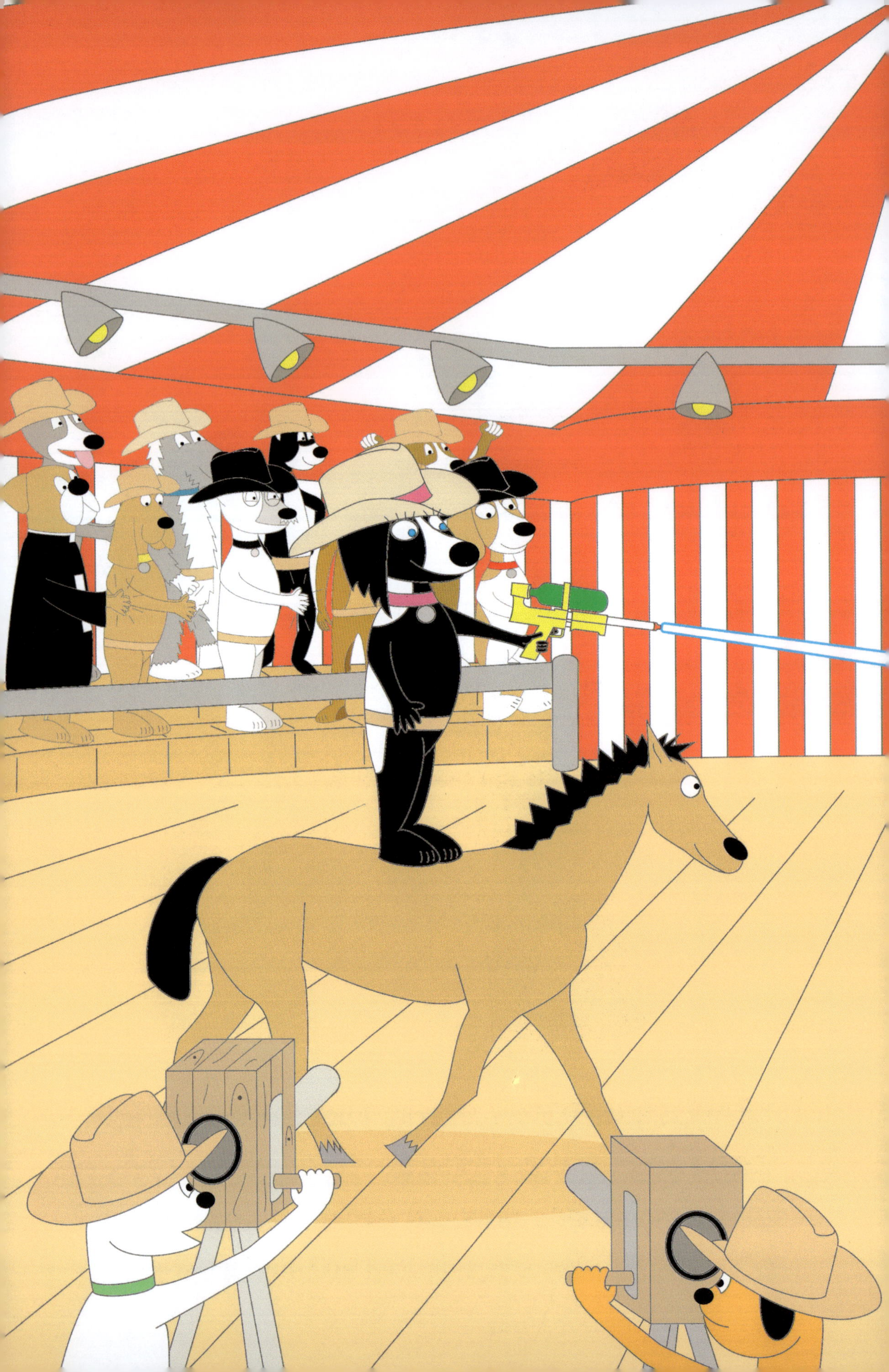

But Annie stole the show with her precise aim,
She could hit a card side on and put out a burning flame,
She could stand atop her horse, shooting from her hips,
Blasting moving objects and even bones from Frank's lips!

Also in the show, was a chief called Sitting Bull, who wanted a photo of Annie, offering a golden purse so full,

"Your skills are supernatural," said the chief respectfully,
"I name you Little Sure Shot, I adopt you, please agree."

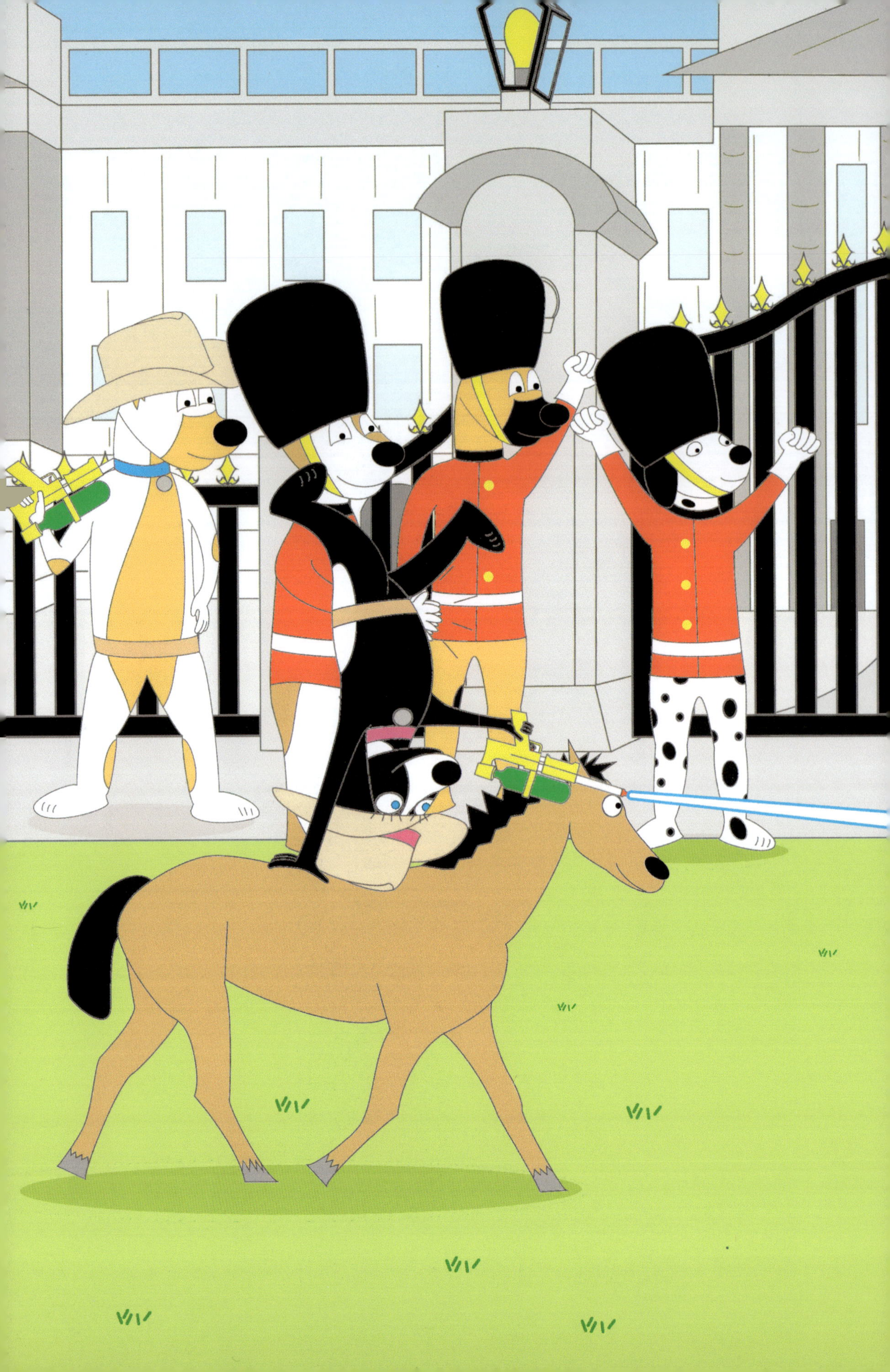

Annie became so famous that the Queen
of England beckoned,
"I wish to see Little Sure Shot shooting
targets down this second!"
So Annie went to England and performed for the
Queen,
As the first famous superstar the world had ever seen!

Printed in Great Britain
by Amazon